The Power of Change Will Heal the Land

Kwabena " Beno" Miller

ISBN-13:
978-1545168950

ISBN-10:
1545168954
:

CONTENTS

Foreword

The Power of Change Will Heal The Land, is a book of help, hope, and healing of the heart. It renders a plethora of wise counsel that will point the reader into their purpose and divine destiny. This book will enlighten you on how Satan can destroy a person's life, yet in a moment of time God can rebuild and restore everything that was broken.

The author has openly used his own personal failures, flaws and poor decisions, as word pictures and examples of how not to live. He willingly chooses to expose the frailties of his journey in hopes of rescuing some man, woman, boy, or girl, from falling off the cliff of destruction.

However, it is not just a book of doom and gloom it is also a book of radical redemption. As you listen to the biography of a young urban man who has made his share of bad mistakes and missed managed moments, yet ultimately was transformed into an agent of change, you will not just see him, but you will also see the potential of your own life. There is no secret about what God can do. What He did for Kwabena he will do for you, or your son, or your grandson.

It has been a privileged to be able to read this wonderful narrative of transformation, but I am even more privileged to have been able to witness it with my own eyes. Beno has been an inspiration, an icon, and a change agent in our city and his testimony has literally saved the lives of countless young people. I am grateful to be called his Pastor. In the Words of the Creator and Sustainer of all things, the only Wise God, " thou art my beloved son whom I am well pleased with".

Daryl Arnold,. Sr. Pastor
Overcoming Believers Church
Knoxville, TN

ACKNOWLEDGMENTS

The Power of Change Will Heal the Land

This book is dedicated to four of the most important people having impacted my life: Vicki Prater, David Miller, Edward Allen Miller, and Pastor Daryl Arnold.

First, my mother, Vicki Prater, for being the vessel used by God to bring me into this world; for providing for me the best that she was capable of giving. I thank God for the knowledge of knowing that she accepted Jesus Christ as her Lord and Savior before she departed this earth.

Secondly, my father, David Miller, for being the carrier of the seed with my name on it; for stepping up and being the best dad he was capable of being at a time that was very critical in my life. I thank God for the knowledge of his salvation as well.

Thirdly, my grandfather, Edward Allen Miller, whose prayers I believe were heard by God; and the Holy Spirit, was sent to bring me into the Kingdom.

Lastly, but by far, not the least of these, is the recognition and thanks I give to my spiritual father, Pastor Daryl Arnold, for mentoring, believing and trusting in me to be the man that God has called me to be. Without his leadership and support, this journey would have been much harder to travel. His continued support as a spiritual father and mentor is valued beyond measure; he is one of a very few, for whom I would willingly take a spiritual bullet.

Introduction

I take a deep breath in this world of sin. When I sit back and think on how the devil (enemy) can take something that is as repulsive as violence and death; and make it look attractive in the hearts and minds of so many people, I am appalled. This book is not written to glorify violence and death, rather to unmask it; to display that there is nothing glorious about it.

This book is written to glorify my Deliverer and my Redeemer. I am taking this time to reflect back on my life in the streets, only to encourage every reader to know that God has the power to deliver anyone, from anything, at any time; no matter where they come from; rich or poor, black or white, saved or unsaved.

There is hope for you; there is also hope for those whom you've given up on. Never underestimate the power of God to change anyone or any circumstance. It seems impossible to us, because for us it is impossible, but God has the ability to walk a camel through the eye of a needle.

So, don't belittle any man, don't force your deliverance on them; instead pray. When you pray for them, speak life over them. Decree and declare that they are blessed and endowed with the power of God to change.

I pray that this book will bless you with insight into a world that may seem foreign to you, but it is reality for so many others. Optimism, is a word used for certain people in certain situations, but I am optimistic that the eyes of your understanding will be opened; that courage to encourage a lost and dying world will overtake you to effect a change at any level that you can.

People only know what they have been taught. They cannot go where they have never been; they cannot teach what they do not know. You know where you have been, but you do not know when you are going. This is enticement to not judge things that you do not understand, rather gain understanding, and then do whatever you can to help influence and advocate for change. It is your choice, so choose wisely; your very life depends on it.

My Prayer for the Lost

"In the name of Jesus Christ, I call forth every lost soul, who reads this book, out of darkness and into the marvelous light. You will prosper in spirit, soul, and body. You shall live and not die to declare the works of the Lord. I pray that God will bless you with an appetite for the word of the Lord that you would gain understanding. May God create in you a new heart that you will hunger after righteousness for righteousness sake. I call you blessed in Jesus name, Amen."

We all have a Choice

I am profoundly excited about being changed, because I know where I've been. The feeling is like I've walked up out of a fire without smelling like smoke; when I deserved to have been burned up; living a life where many people do not make it out alive. Some lose their mind or get sentence to life in prison before they truly learn anything about life. How many did not make the change, not because they couldn't, but because they chose not to -- trapped, not by another man, neither by any circumstance, but by the vanity in their own mind? Back in high school, when we thought we knew it all. If you grew up in the projects we didn't have many advantages, but we all had a choice. Rather rich or poor; the power to choose, without the wisdom to use it, can be a snare. We thought we had all the sense back then; but failed to realize that a portion of that sense was the ability to make good choices; we all had a choice. We could have stayed in school and applied ourselves, or choose to go to work in the erroneous economy.

Low income neighborhoods around the world have always engineered their own economic systems to get out of the hole, to get ahead. Some call it the game, some call it street life, regardless, it's all a hustle. The game is a business just like any other enterprise. Some of the smartest people I know just made bad choices and furthered the wrong economy.

If we would have grinded in school like we did in the streets there would be more jobs instead of more prisons. I am not going to make excuses for my decisions. I am one of those who boosted the wrong economy. Like brother Westfield, one of my most fierce enemies in the streets said, "I've been wrong for too long.' If you've been wrong for too long; I pray God Almighty you're older and wiser now; and that by the grace of God you have lived through it.

By now you've heard wisdom raise her voice over and over. In some way every day lady wisdom go out in the streets and shout do not come this way. You can hear her speak when you see a man 50 years old and the only thing he ever owned is a jail cell; you can hear her speak when you see a man go three days without eating cause he chasing a high that has been running for thirty years, but the worst is seeing a broken hearted mother or father staring at their dead child, lying in a pool of blood after being shot down in the streets. If you've seen any of this then you have seen enough to know that there has to be a change and that change starts with you. God is blessing you so that you may be a blessing to others, to show them the way out of the life.

With your experience you can be the wisdom a young child needs to make the right choices before they go amiss. We already know the options and the possibilities of the outcome. We have seen it all before.

Although it looks attractive on television and sounds good in music, we know the truth of an ugly reality. The mind is a battlefield where the enemy plants thoughts, ideas, and suggestions that can have a young mind, motivated and inspired by faulty dreams that are a set up for their demise. He used the same tricks with us when we were children, because we were young, immature and simple minded.

When I was a child I thought like a child, I spoke like a child, I reasoned like a child, but when I became a man I put childish ways behind me. (1 Corinthians 13:11). Only then could I hear from God. It was then that I could see the plan of the enemy for an entire generation.

When I put off being a real nigga and became a real man, in heart, mind and spirit, I began to love according to the knowledge of His word. Now, if you lack understanding you may use the term sell-out, to describe who I have become; but it is funny how the people who need change the most, give intelligent change a bad rap.

Understand, if I would not have transformed when I did, there would be more Bloods and Crips dead today; there would be more Gangster Disciples and Vice Lords dead today; not because I would have physically killed them, but because I learned to wage a different type of warfare. I had a new weapon. The prayers of the righteous availeth much. That is called loving according to righteous knowledge. I learned how to pray for people.

Don't get it twisted, you're not still walking around because of your reputation. You're not cut like that, for real. If God had removed his hand from you, the deceiver would have crushed you a long time ago.

Indeed, God is patient, not wanting any of us to perish; but understand no one is exempt. We all have a choice. Choose wisely, someone is counting on you. Deuteronomy 30:19 says "I call heaven and earth to witness against you today, that I have set before you life and death, the blessing and the curse. So you choose life in order that you may live; you and your descendants.

Inside the Home

I know that people from diverse backgrounds and various walks of life will read this book. It is important that they know and understand that some of the things that go on inside the projects and low income housing have a direct effect on the epidemic of gang violence, drug use, and drug dealing across this entire country.

Innocent children are dying; some are growing up motherless, fatherless and in some cases both. These children turn to dope for hope; and to gangs for acceptance. Many of them could have become professionals or skilled workers from every genre of life; working taxpayers contributing to a stronger American economy.

Instead they are in penitentiaries deteriorating; dead; or on drugs. I hope God Himself, not me, has put it in your heart to *help heal the land*. He has blessed you in some way to be a blessing to someone else. It could be an anointing to pray, to give, to lead, or to serve. Whatever it is; we are all stronger together than we are apart.

I can tell my story better than anyone else can. I know what went on in my home, so I'll just give a brief back story about my family.

I was born to a single mother, Vicki Prater, living in low income project apartments within the city. As a youth we moved to different projects throughout the Knoxville area. Deep inside my heart, I believe God purposed things to happen that way. I wouldn't trade the experiences for anything. I have memories I will always cherish.

Mostly, I was raised up in East Knoxville. Playing football with the Baby Road Runners is how I started off developing my childhood friendship base. My dad's name is David Miller we both have similar stories, we just lived them out in different generations.

I have an older sister, Yahphett Truman Robinson and a brother that is one year younger than me, named Gary Miller. Some people call him G-nut. I used to call him that too, but I have renounced doing so, since I've learned that death and life is in the power of the tongue; and that you can frame a person's life by what you call them. (Proverbs

18:21).

There are some instances in the bible where God changed the names of the people He called. Abram became Abraham, Simon became Peter and Saul became Paul. There is power in the names and labels that you proclaim upon yourself and power behind the names and labels that people declare upon you.

From the first time I can remember being conscious of us staying in the projects, it was my mother my sister, me and my brother. Even though we lived in the projects it didn't feel like we were poor. My mother always kept the place clean and she made sure there was a meal on the table every day. It may have been fried cornbread and beans, but with hot sauce, it tasted as good as any other meal in the world to me.

Life wasn't that bad. If we were not eating at home, we would be at the center eating go-go boxes and running around the projects playing some kind of game. We were not dodging bullets back then, but we were fighting all the time; even if you didn't want to fight, you had to fight to make it.

Violence was ever-present. Sometimes, I wonder if the enemy used hand-to-hand combat to desensitize us to bloodshed at a young age. He provided a gateway for death by your own hands. Violence begets violence is a partial quote taken from a speech made by the late Dr. Martin Luther King, Jr. in 1958.

It was in the mid-80s when all hell broke out in our home. Trouble hit my mother harder than anyone first; that's around the time when hard drugs invaded our communities. The problems we see today all started with drugs not gangs.

By now, we all know the famous saying that the love of money is the root of all evil. It seemed the drug of choice went from weed to cocaine, needles and crack pipes.

For my mother, it all started off with bad relationships. My mother's downfall were the men she allowed into her life. My mother was doing better when she was single. For years the only thing she would do when she partied on the weekends was smoke weed, drink coolers, and listen to the gap band, Morris day, Michael Jackson and several other groups that were popular during those times.

One of those weekends she met a clean, smooth talking brother from Alabama. They had good party chemistry and wanted it to continue into a relationship. Now, I don't want to embarrass anyone by putting them on blast, so in this book I'll just call him Michael Myers. This man had a problem with his hands, but that did not stop my mother from marrying him. It should've, but it didn't. They fought before the marriage and after. He even knocked her gold tooth out.

One day they started fighting while I was in the house. I heard my mother call out for help, so I ran to her voice. I grabbed his leg, but he kicked me off. She said go and call the police! I was confused. I didn't want to leave her but she kept saying go call the police. So, I took off as fast as I could.

The project building we stayed in sat on a hill. I lost my balance and went tumbling down the hill. When I got to the bottom I rolled back into position and kicked into a sprint. Back then phones were not that popular, so I ran right over 300 yards until I about fell out, but I made it to a phone. They had a nasty breakup, so he moved back to Alabama.

It wasn't long before my mother started to miss him. He told my mother he had gotten established in his hometown; that he had his own place and we could stay with him. So, we packed up to move to Birmingham, Alabama. When we reached our destination; we pulled up to a white box shaped, straight-up shack. This place made the projects look like luxury condominiums.

We lost it; we were bamboozled. He had gotten us down here in this mess. When it rained we had buckets throughout the house to catch the water to keep it from soaking the floor. The plumbing didn't work either, so I knew what it would be like to go outside to use the restroom; like the old days. Worst of all the rats in the shack were large. I could not stand the sound of those rats.

They never let up. Every night I could hear them scratching and screeching inside the walls. The rat traps sounded like small hand guns. I never went back to sleep after waking up from one of those things going off.

I always made sure I used the restroom before I went

to bed and I never drank anything late in the evening, so I would not have to get out of bed in the middle of the night to use the restroom. It was pitch black dark. I could not see anything. All I could do is hear rats. I had a vivid imagination; that invented, if I got out of the bed, a big rat would lock onto my toe as soon as it touched the floor.

In spite of all of this, during the hardest times of our lives, mama made sure we ate every day. There was only one evening we missed a meal. Mama was at the table crying. I remember asking mama several times, why can't you just go back to being single? Thank God, there comes a time when every woman gets fed up.

One day my mama came home late, she was bringing some groceries through the door. As she walked through the door she started, calling our names out, one at a time; from the oldest to the youngest. By the time she got to Gary's name and before she could finish saying it, he hit her, knocking her down. We heard her screaming and the sound of groceries falling onto the floor. From that point on, it's like I had a blackout. I can't remember anything else concerning him. I just know that was their last day together.

We came back one last time to get our stuff out of that shack, but we were not alone; outside of that door, stood a tall man with broad shoulders. When Michael Myers opened the door, the tall man looked him square in the eyes, like a man, and told him, "she is coming to get all of her stuff and you better not touch her." Michael Myers had a stunned facial expression, but he didn't go crooked. He stepped aside and let us in.

Now that was impressive to me; after that incident, I looked up to this man like he was my hero. I called him our new friend. Finally I felt like we were safe. Here is someone who can protect my mama and take care of us. It felt like we were in good hands when he stood up for my mama.

I was wrong; all wrong. He was worse, no he was **THE** worst. I will call him Freddy Krueger. We had no idea my mama was about to walk into the darkest time of her life. Freddy Krueger was the neighborhood drug dealer.

You see the problem back then is that a lot of drug dealers started getting high on their own supply; crossing over from weed to cocaine and shooting up. From the look of things he would be the one to introduce my mama to the needle.

I came home one day from Thompson Elementary School. I jumped off the bus rushing home excited to show my mama the cloths my school teacher brought me to school.

Evidently I ran into something I wasn't supposed to see. At the time I didn't realize what it was. I just knew that it didn't seem right. Freddy Krueger was holding my mama's arm with one hand and pushing a needle in it with the other hand. Mama looked up and saw me staring at her. She told me to go back to my room. I had to walk past her to get to my room; on the way into my room, I overheard Freddy Krueger tell my mama to be still Vickie. That's all I can remember about that precise situation; it's all I care to remember about it.

Our time in Alabama didn't last long it was right at a year. The final days came about after mom started getting physically abused again. After coming home one day from

playing around the neighborhood I noticed the glass screen door was shattered. I walked in to see my big sister crying. I asked what happened. She said mama is
in the hospital. Freddy Krueger beat her with a pipe and broke her arm.

I remember hating Freddy Krueger even more than I hated the previous man. It pained me to see my mama go through all this hurting and suffering at the hands of men that were supposed to care for her. They didn't care about her having children or the impact their abuse of her was having on her children; and I couldn't even protect her.

This was it for mama she was ready to leave Freddy Krueger and get out of this nightmare. As soon as she got out of the hospital, she called grandmamma to ask her if she could help her get back to Knoxville. With my grandparents help we made it back to Knoxville.

The following year, walking out of my bedroom I found my mother OD'd in her bedroom, her friends were around her panicking. It looked like her eyes were open but she wasn't moving. The whole thing looked scary. I just started yelling get up mama get up. Crying, my big cousin, Barry took me back in my room and said he got her; your mama is ok.

A little later that night I came back out the room looking for mama. I went down the steps and peeped around the corner when she spotted my head and started walking towards me. Her eyes were so big I thought she was a spirit. I was a little spooked out; she bent down to kiss me. I pulled back with my eyes locked on her eyes to see if she was really alright according to my little understanding. She said, "I love you. Go to bed and get some rest."

I did what she said. I went to bed. When I woke up the next morning mama was gone; for three days she was absent from us. This was the beginning of a pattern that soon became obvious. Evidently, the drug addiction that started in Alabama followed mama back up here to Knoxville.

Every month mama would be gone for days sometimes a week. My sister was just 12 years old. She stepped up like a big girl to make sure we ate every day.

This went on for months, until one day Gary got sick and Yahphett didn't know what to do so she called grandmamma. My Grandmamma got in touch with my dad and told him them kids don't have nobody staying with them and Gary is sick can you do something.

Dad came to pick Gary up and took him to the hospital. They found that he had pneumonia. The next day mama came back home. I'm not sure what was said, but they exchanged words and dad left.

Mama got noticeably worse, she started losing weight. One day she left home and did not come back. My dad did not like the sudden change in responsibility, but he was too much of a man to leave us in the situation we were in. He had a relative that was disputing whether we were his children or not. Emotionally the transition was rough.

Still to this day, I have two birth certificates; one is an old terminated copy with my sister's dad's name on it. These events felt like a dark cloud of rejection made its home in my head. I developed a bad attitude. I believe resentment started to hide itself in my heart. I didn't want it there, but I couldn't stop the hurt and the frustration. I wasn't mature enough to explain myself; to help anyone understand what was going on inside of me. Before I even became a man the enemy tried to stunt my growth.

Right after the fifth grade that summer I ran away and moved in with my cousin, Penny in Greenhill's. I always behaved well with her because she made me feel special. I didn't tell her I ran away, I just moved in. I was over there every day anyways so nobody could tell. I thought I was smooth, till one day I was walking down McCalla Avenue and my grandmamma caught me slippin.. She said, "Hey boy, come here", I started to take off running; that's what my mind said to do, but my feet froze up on me. She asked me if I needed a ride home and I told her no. She said come on I will give you a ride anyway I'm going that way, I couldn't say no or explain to her I ran away, so I just got in the car and went back home.

By the end of the summer before my sixth grade year started, my mama got her an apartment. So, we moved back in with her. She did good for a year, after that the drugs started to become overpowering again. So we moved back in with dad. By this time home was just a place I laid my head.

My dad tried harder to make a difference, but I was just rebellious. I was always in the streets; that's where the love was at and you couldn't tell me any different. Around the time I was finishing up with middle school my dad moved out to the country. I would take the homies from the hood out there. Everyone and I mean everybody, would trip on how deep that house set off in the woods.

The driveway went about 100 yards off into the woods before you reached the house. I kind of liked it out there. At first it was something new, but I wasn't favored out there. One day my dad and one of his friends were around the house having a couple of drinks.

The man looked up and pointed at me and said, "You see this one right here? He is going to be dead before he turns 18." It seemed like he had my dad persuaded that what he said was true. That's what upset me the most. My dad was not argumentative.

It took a lot to get him upset, but I felt that should have upset him. I couldn't figure out why he said that. I wasn't the best child, but I was respectful toward my elders. I had never done anything to this man. So I asked, "Why is he tripping?"

When I think about it now, I say he would have been right if God's hand wasn't on me. Based on statistics his prediction was likely to happen, but he just didn't know that Jesus Christ died to save a wretch like me over 2000 years ago.

To analyze what he said; look back at my world. They say home is where your heart is. Your world is limited to what you see around you every day. My heart was in the hood and I didn't think outside that box and in my world, guns and drugs were more abundant than anything else. Almost every young person's mom or dad was on some kind of drug if not both parents.

Almost every young person had a gun, a temper and an ego to go along with it. I had a gun before I had an education. Before I made it out of high school I was on bond waiting to go to the penitentiary for a violent charge. My lawyer explained to me a diploma would be favorable for me when I go to court for sentencing.

It was too late for me to get back in high school, but I was able to get a homebound teacher to help me catch up and get a special education diploma. When I walked across the stage, I had more schoolmates gasping in disbelief, than I had cheering me on.

Although, I walked across that stage; I still walked right into the penitentiary months later with the same sentence. Could prison be God's way of shielding me from a premature death; and why did it take prison for me to take a high school diploma seriously?

Why does something that is as great as an education, lose its value in the hearts and minds of many young people in low income housing across this nation? I can tell you from my perspective, working in the wrong economy. You have to envision yourself being something that needs an education.

A lot of the people I grew up with didn't think they would ever need an education; but to a person, I have not run into anyone of them today that did not regret that decision later on. At the time school was interfering with the hustle. You didn't need a diploma to buy cocaine. You didn't need a license to buy guns where I'm from.

I, along with so many others actually thought the best way to success was hustling up on a kilogram of cocaine. If I could just reach a kilo I would be successful. I did not feel like it was wrong to sell crack. In our prevalent way of thinking the ends justified the means. It was just too normal to be wrong.

Like gangs are today, they are too popular for children not to be tempted to want to get down. I just thought it was wrong to get caught; survival of the slickest. It didn't occur to me that this is the same poison Freddy Krueger used to destroy my mother's life and take her from her kids. In no way did I have sensitivity to human life; just numbed by a lustful mindset toward money; to get mine. Have I become the man I hated the most, Freddy Krueger? The resemblance was overpowering; someone's parents were smoking their children's welfare check, with my supply.

Mercy

If you are trying to reach someone to keep them from going astray; understanding is important. Acceptance or belonging is one of the essential needs of human beings, according to Maslow's theory. It does not matter where the person is from, a need to belong is critical to healthy development. Too many grown men are disguising that rational child-like desire behind their fear of rejection. The fear of rejection is real. The issue may seem small, but there's a 50-50 chance that the absence of belonging can progress into some big problems.

I believe the best way to reach someone is to show them the same mercy we have received and still need from God. You might feel like you wouldn't have ever made that particular mistake; perhaps you would not have, just try to understand what could have led them to their decisions; without making a right or wrong judgement about it. Chances are you have never been in their situation.

Having a life advantage does not make you better; we all fall short in some kind of way. That's why when we get up, we lean forward to extend a helping hand upward to the other person. That's the kind of grace I have inside of me; having been forgiven for the mistakes that I made. I've learned how to give it back.

I know I'm not blessed because I'm so wonderful; I am that man that got it wrong over and over again. I passionately followed a path that left me with nothing but a cry to God. All I had was a cry, nothing else and no one else, but through Jesus Christ alone, I was recovered. I'm in debt to no man. But I owe it to God to make the gospel relevant to every man. Whether I have to come down or come up to meet him where he's at, I can unabashedly, speak compassion to the unattractive weak.

Understand, grown men don't join gangs, children do, but the love and the unity are so attractive it can attract even a grown man. So many come in as a child and never get out even if they are fortunate enough to get old. I did not join a gang because I was tough or a killer; not even because I hated anybody from another side of town. It was a three-fold cord that pulled me in, the love, unity, and acceptance; all-natural human needs.

Lord knows, when I went to the penitentiary and did my first bid; it carried the faithfulness of a religion. I had a purpose now, something I lived for. I had sacrificed my soul to it. Love for my homies led me to a hard heart toward their enemies, even if I never met them before. If anyone wished to do harm to my brothers, then I became a threat to them, even if it cost me my life.

There were many other men with identical hearts, from different gangs, ready for battle, if the war should jump off. No guns in the penitentiary, only hand-to-hand combat. The average arm was 18 inches. If you didn't have them, somebody in your set had 20 inch arms.

Like the Avengers everybody had a Hulk on their team. The Gangster Disciples', Crips, Vice Lords, Bloods and the Aryan brotherhoods were the most common gangs; and all of them were forces to be reckoned with. I had a fight with somebody from every gang, except my own. With an air of tension always present, some penitentiaries would be like a war zone. Sometimes I had to take a shower with my knife in one hand and soap in the other.

I've seen it before. If somebody open up that shower and start sticking you, you would not have time to reach for your knife. Those few seconds it took to find your knife could be a matter of your life or death. The plan is to try to catch you with soap in your eyes. You have to do your best to push that blade in them before they get one in you.

Some penitentiaries were not as bad as others; no matter what penitentiary you were sent to do your time, nobody left the penitentiary the same way they came in. Either you leave a better man or you leave worse, depending on how you choose to do your time.

During my first eight year bid in the state I grew worse. Every time I went in, I came out doing the same crimes better. It appeared my chances to excel in life were more achievable by getting better at doing wrong; than it would be trying to do right... but God. What I mean by that is *but* God had His hand on me. You see, He never did let me stay in the streets long with my state of mind. The first time I made parole I stayed out for three months, the next time two months. Parole officers didn't cut me any breaks.

After Christmas of 1994 until 2006 I was only in the free world for a total of 14 months. Penitentiary was God's way of shielding me from death and keeping me from killing someone. 2001 was the longest time I was out. In 9 months I had over $70,000 in cocaine go through my hands. In one month I blew $20,000 snorting cocaine all night through the week. I knew every powder head in the hood undercover or wide open, male or female I knew them all.

When I ate (increased) my homies ate with me. I loved being able to feed the homies. Money and dope came easy for me I robbed any drug dealer I wanted to when I wanted to, without a mask, because I knew they couldn't tell the police I took their dope and money.

Instead they would have to bring it to the streets. That's the message I wanted to get across, that, *the streets were ours*. I was so close to death and so far from God. That is a terrible reality; nobody wants to see the end of that road.

It was as if God rescued me through incarceration. King David said it himself in Psalms 119:71 "it was good for me to be afflicted so that I might learn your decrees."

I was locked up on the night of the ninth month out of the penitentiary. One of my closest brothers was gunned down that night. I was the supposed target. A week later I made bond, but the next day I was indicted by the Fed's. They sent me to Blount County jail in Maryville, Tennessee.

This county jail abounded with ministers who covered that place twice a week. When they came into the pod to minister you could either go in your cell or stay out in the dayroom and listen to them. Now, I've never been one to oppose the gospel, I wasn't a fool. I always believed there was a God. I heard about Jesus many times as a child. I just simply was not attracted to Jesus, until I came to realize how much I really needed Him.

A tall white man walked into our dayroom to share the word with us. They actually locked him in the dayroom with us. He couldn't go anywhere for an entire hour. I had already done my push-ups for the day, so after reasoning, I figured

I'd stay out and listen to what the man had to say. He looked like he actually cared; like he was glad to be here talking with us. His disposition was inspiring.

What he had looked more attractive than my current situation. In no way did he come across as if I was any less significant than him. I will never forget this brother. I didn't have the friendliest demeanor, but he was comfortable engaging with me. He talked about the mercy of God. Lord knows, I needed that. It's funny how we think something is for the weak until we need it for ourselves.

Showing mercy is weakness; is a lie. It came from the father of lies. It is nothing but a trick of the enemy to make violence and mayhem look glorious. Tell me who can compare to God in strength? None can come close; yet He is full of mercy. It is obvious that our whole value system is disordered, when what we thought of as being weak; is really being strong.

No love and no mercy equal no God; no God equals no hope. Understand that the enemy can transform himself into an angel of light according to (2 Corinthians 11:14), so he knows how to make wrong look right, weak look attractive and he can have a man glorifying ignorance like it's the truth.

On this day mercy sounds sweet because I need it. My sins were staring me in the face and it felt good knowing that in spite of me, I am still loved and accepted by an Almighty God, who I had violated over and over again. I became more sensitive to my wrongs than I had ever been in my life.

Just two weeks prior, one of my brothers was gunned down for something he did not have anything to do with. I'm not saying he was an innocent man, but this time that bullet was meant for me; it was my beef; instead, someone close to me died behind my actions. That brother was my dude; when you see me you would see him. Indeed, the love is real, even if it was misguided love; the blind leading the blind down a dark path.

When I got alone in my cell I began to do some serious reflection. I thought back on my life up until the present. It didn't feel like I had even lived yet. I had been in and out of this jail life since I was 18. I had never been in love, I never had any children, never had my own place; I hadn't been anywhere except the hood and the penitentiary with these hard ankles all around me. For so many, this is all they will ever see. No one is to blame for my situation, but me.

I took ownership and said God my life is not right because I haven't been living right. A hunger for change came over me. I wanted it, but I knew I couldn't do it on my own. I got on my knees and I cried out to God. It wasn't a tranquil request. I begin to wet the floor with my tears. I petitioned God with these exact words, "God forgive me for all the wrong I've done. I don't want to continue on like this. You said that if I believe in Jesus Christ you will hear my prayer. I believe that Jesus Christ died for my sins. I believe that He rose from the dead; now I ask that you change me, make me a better man, I want to be a strong man spiritually, mentally, and physically."

Not one time did I ask God to let me out; I didn't feel like I deserved to get out. I just wanted to change. I thought the results I wanted would happen immediately. I was so inspired, I figured I'd get up and do everything the right way instantaneously. It didn't work out that way. What came straightaway was an appetite for the word of God. I got up from my knees wanting to read; I became a bookworm. The next day when the Chaplain came through with the book cart, I bum rushed him, trying to be the first one to get what I wanted.

Reaching through the bars I started flipping through books like they had gold in them. As I'm reading the Bible, I actually understand what I'm reading and the understanding is making me want more. I could read for hours and not get bored with the Word. I loved talking about what I learned in the Bible, so I'm telling everybody around me.

One Crip I was real cool with, on the town, asked me a question; by the way he was a powder head too. On some nights in the club, when that cocaine came out, snorters from every hood would be in the bathroom on a peace treaty called getting high. We started off getting cool over a snort pact. He said, "Beno what about Blood, now that you're saved are you still a Blood?" I held up my hand and said, "I'm still black right, just like being saved doesn't stop me from being a black man, so it doesn't stop me from being a Blood, It's Blood for life."

I would soon find out what needed to change and how far I had to go to affect that change. It seemed like the only thing that actually changed is that I hated doing wrong; but I still did it. For example, I managed to get some men together for Bible study in the dayroom. We formed a circle and I started talking about the bible but it only lasted ten minutes, because I ended up getting into a fight with an outlaw biker over some disagreement. After he got up he slammed his bible up against the wall. It was as if he slammed my own heart against the wall. I felt terrible afterwards.

Here it is I'm supposed to be helping someone, but I end up making him worse. I thought to myself I'm trying to do right but I can't get it together. Frustrated with myself, I said to God, "not even You can change me. I'm just a thug for life. So why even try."

The fact that I hated the wrong I did was evidence that I was a changed man. I didn't know it at the time, but the enemy was using condemnation to kill my hope of being the man I wanted to be. I did not understand the process. It does not matter how old you are in the natural, when you are freshly born again, you are a baby spiritually. You cannot expect a baby to have the strength of a young man and a young man does not have the wisdom of a father. However, from birth to death the blood of Jesus trumps every sin we will ever commit. It is hard for us to forgive ourselves sometimes, but it's never a problem for Him to forgive us.

I remember sitting in that same cell where I first cried out to God. Now I am sitting here feeling defeated, ready to retire and I have only been saved two weeks. He spoke to me in an audible voice. It came from inside of me right where my heart is, but I heard it with my ears. He said, "Why are you always thinking? Stop thinking; conquer with your heart and not your brain."

Immediately, I knew it was God, so I jumped off my bunk with excitement; not about what He said, but about the fact that God spoke to me in an audible voice. I heard Him as clear as day, inside of me. Then I sat back down and gave thought to what He said. If you are like me you may wonder why in the world God would tell me to stop thinking. I didn't understand it then; but I wrote on paper, what God said word for word. I locked it in my memory by meditating on it. Supernaturally, hearing from God like that provoked me to keep reading until I found out why He said that to me. I was determined to get it, and now I have it to share with you.

Understand that the mind is a battlefield where the enemy wages war upon us with his weapons of thoughts, ideas, and suggestions. I speak about thoughts that are planted in your mind by the enemy. I, being a thug for life was not in the bible, but those thoughts were in my mind and those thoughts came from the enemy, not God. God does not covenant with our mind. He speaks to our heart and what he puts in our heart we use to get our mind in check. Three specific scriptures speak to us about renewing our minds daily, Romans 12:1-2, Philippians 4:8-9, and Hebrews 3:1.

When the Lord spoke to me, He used the word conquer. According to Miriam Webster, conquer means to take by force. So when the Lord said conquer with your heart and not your brain, He is saying, use the word I put in your heart to run the enemy up out of your mind. Do not let the enemy use your brain to ruin what I'm doing in you.

I was allowing my brain to lead when it was no longer fit to be the captain. Faith is a heart matter. Jesus Christ's covenant with us was written on the tablet of our heart. We use our faith to change our thinking. It is important that we do not allow thinking to abort faith. It is also important that we run a check on our mind daily. What we think about ourselves should align with what God knows about us. If he gives you a word and you believe contrary to that word, then, that God word will not manifest in your life because you're allowing yourself to be held captive by your thinking; trapped by the vanity in your own mind.

What the people of God need is a mind alignment to keep them on the straight and narrow path. Parallel your thinking with the word of God, so when the enemy comes with those thoughts, ideas and suggestions, which are not in line with the word of God you can run him up out your space with the word of God. The presence of God's word in your thought life will preserve your very life and your destiny.

God spoke this word to me 16 years ago in a jail cell and I am just now getting the revelation as I am writing this book in my house. A lot has changed in me since then, but I still have so far to go.

He carried me as a baby, but now I'm a man of God. He has greater expectations of me. Now he is saying, in order to make it to the next level we can no longer be passive. We must take authority; gain dominion over other areas of our lives that are not yet submitted to the will of God. Fight the good fight of faith, conquer with your heart. (1 Timothy 6:12).

Shots Fired From the Past

I got in that Word and I have not put it down since. Reading is what changed my life. If your mind never changes, then your life will never change. The best analogy to describe the importance of reading for transformation is by using a computer. After being in darkness for so long my mind was like a computer that had to be rebooted. It had to be deprogrammed from chaos and reprogrammed by the word of God. That is why I do not understand how someone can change without reading or listening to the Word.

When I read the Bible it takes out what the world put in me, what street life instilled in me; lies that accumulated throughout my life; replacing them with truth and virtues. The word of God is like a vacuum that sucks out darkness. The truth takes up residence, evicting all lies. My growth became more noticeable as I began to walk with more humility. I began to pursue peace with men in the manner by which I carried myself.

A couple of years into my sentence my past started

putting me on Front Street. One of the older guys from Knoxville had noticed the change in me. He had been watching my walk. We talked about the Bible from time to time. One day Hank said, "Beno it's easy to make that change in here man, but what about when you get on the streets. You still have enemies out there that haven't changed and don't care about your change. Remember that day you got into a fight with my nephew at the penal farm. When you left the pod he told us when he see you on the street he is not going to say anything to you he's just going to walk up to you and shoot you in the face."

Hank wasn't trying to be discouraging, those were just the type of conversations we had. That's how we conversed; real talk. Although the message was discouraging, he was raising my awareness; at the same time wanting to know what do you do in that kind of situation. I was lost for a minute, the information made me feel threatened.

The shots to the face had me visualizing a closed casket or living with a fractured face. I was a youth in Christ.

I did not understand that I did not have to kill, to save

my own life. I yield my life to Christ; and what He has use for He keeps. When it is my time I will face death with man-like faith. I replied, "I don't know Hank, I don't want any trouble, but I can't let your nephew get out on me. It will not just be that easy for him." This became a legitimate concern to me. I'm wondering what this could lead to. I don't want that kind of life anymore. So, when I got in my cell I got on my knees and asked God about it, "Father, what do I do in this situation you said pursue peace with all men. What about my enemies that haven't change and may try to come for my life? Do I need to carry a gun and a Bible? One day I will have to face the streets again, Lord, you said I can come to you for whatever I need, so I put this in your hands in Jesus name I pray amen."

My God is sovereign and Lord over all. There is no situation He cannot fix. About a week after this prayer I was reading the book of Proverbs when I came across this word Proverbs 16:7 when a man's ways please the Lord, he makes even his enemies to be at peace with him.

When I read this Scripture I knew it was God

answering my prayers. Right then I received it and said thank you Lord. To me this meant so much because I wanted a change in life. To change your life you have to change your ways. A fool is a magnet for trouble, but it is hard to have strife with a humbled man.

I saw this man, who allegedly was going to shoot me in my face, three months after my release. We met eye to eye at a store. I asked him how was he doing he responded by saying I'm doing well; congratulations on your change man I wish you the best. I said thank you blessed man and I pray blessing upon you as well. We shook hands and hugged one another. That was God fulfilling his word.

It wasn't long after that, my past took another shot at me. I am halfway through my sentences when I get shackled up and shipped back down to Knoxville to get booked for murder. I remember sitting in a room with several state detectives around me.

The black one came forward and said. "Kwabena Miller, alias Beno, you know what you're here for? We know what you did, so tell us why did you kill him." I said kill what, who? He said, "We have 11 witnesses ready to testify that you killed John Doe in (place) back in (Date)." I said they made that up. I was in the penal farm when that happened. I made bond two days after his murder.

They looked at each other with disappointment then left out the room. I sat there thinking to myself, my God, had I not been locked up when that happened, I would be doing life for a murder, guilty or not guilty. Talk about a blessing in disguise; thank God I was locked up that day. I started giving glory to God and thanking him for his hand of protection. Boy, I tell you, it is in your best interest to love God. Romans 8:28 (KJV) and we know that all things work together for good to them that love God, to them who are the called according to his purpose.

Tearing Down Idols

One day I was in my cell reading (Jeremiah 25: 1-14) about the fall of Jerusalem. The nation of Israel was beaten, and driven from their land into captivity. Their destruction made them an object of repulsion and their cries brought no pity. The king of Babylon killed their young males with the sword. He didn't even spare the young women. The few he did not kill; he bound them into slavery. The beautiful Promised Land, flowing with milk and honey, was laid waste and desolate.

All this happened because Israel rebelled against their God; the only God. They left their God, who had delivered them from slavery in Egypt, to serve false gods that could not deliver them from anything. Their own hands did not make them great. They not once, had power to deliver themselves from any of their oppressors.

From the beginning it was always God; It was God, Jehovah Nissi; the Lord thy Banner who brought them out of Egypt with wealth (Exodus 17:15); and defeated the

Amalekites; It was God who parted the Red Sea so they could walk across on dry land; It was God who swallowed up Pharaoh's Army in the Red the sea; It was God who fed them and gave them water from a rock in the wilderness; It was God who imploded the walls of Jericho so they could possess that land; It was God who gave them the promised land; It was God who defeated their enemies trying to take their land. It was always God and no one else.

As long as Israel served Jehovah, they were a mighty nation, none could come against them, absolutely, no one. God revealed himself to the world through His mighty acts of wonder and majesty on behalf of Israel. There is no other God like Him.

Israel, given the greatest honor ever bestowed upon any nation, was chosen to be a separated people; separated to serve the only true and living God. They were to separate themselves from the worship of pagan gods. Instead of reverencing their chosen status as a people, they sold God out time and again. The Lord God Almighty gave them a firm warning, so that they may keep their ways prosperous. He commanded them saying, "I am the Lord; that is my name! I will not give my glory to another, neither my praise to graven images. (Isaiah 42:8). I am a jealous God; do not put any other gods before me. I will punish up to the third and fourth generation." (Exodus 20:5)

After reading this, I sat in that cell thinking to myself, now, I can understand struggling with sex before marriage or something like that, but this commandment, that should have been an easy one to keep since there is no other God that can do what He do. That's why they call them false gods because they are all fake! Israel must be full of dummies to fall for that one. Right then, is when I heard God say, "you have a false god." I knew instantly what He was talking about! It was Blood. I had enough word in me to understand what God was saying to me. It's called idolatry.

Anything you love more than God is an idol. Anything you worship is your god (it could even be you); anything first in your life, if it is not God, it's an idol.

Anything you practice putting before the word of God, you're idolizing. All of these idols are called false gods they are sitting on the throne in your heart as number one. In doing this, you leave no room for God, because He is, second to none.

God alone sits on the throne; you cannot put Him anyplace else. If He does not sit on the throne of your heart, then you have a false god that cannot deliver. Putting things and people before the word of God can be dangerous. It's like playing musical chairs you might get the seat several times, but you know that eventually you will be the one that misses the beat and then you're out. Let me explain how a man can put something before the word of God.

1) If the word of God says pursue peace with all men; but for some reason you're mean and vengeful

2) If the word of God says love your enemies; but for some reason you keep justifying your hatred.

3) If the word of God says do not kill. (Murder); but for some reason you kill a man unlawfully.

Whatever that reason is, you are exalting your mindset above the word of God, and it is keeping you from observance of the word of God. That reason, that thing, that whatever it is that you idolize, has become your god. The problem with that is, no one can deliver you but Jesus. So you are left with a god that cannot deliver.

I said, "Father that means there are people serving and worshiping false gods everywhere. How did it get like this? We're all just like Israel." Then I went back to the beginning. The reason I joined a gang in my youth was for the trifecta effect; For the love, the acceptance, and for a sense of purpose, all natural human needs that can be assisted by people but completed only by a relationship with a supernatural God.

The reason we are like this is because God put that desire in us for His purpose. God loves us. He has accepted us in Christ. He has a purpose for us in Christ. If unity is something you love, then understand, God loves it even more. Are you willing to unite for the right reason, for His glory and not yours? Are you willing to give Him your heart and let Him reign supreme?

This supernatural God has something that He desires from us. There is a need we all have that is greater than every need. We all have a yearning to worship something; that is what we were created to do. God wants us to come to recognition, a choice, if you will, to worship Him; in spirit and in truth. Worship is what our supernatural God yearns for from us.

Lucifer, the seal of perfection, full of wisdom and perfect in beauty; knows all too well what God purposed us for, because Lucifer, himself, was created to worship, in fact, he was the archangel of praise and worship. He comprehends very well that we are created to be his replacement. He was created by God just as all angels were, but his role was different from the other angelic hosts...Lucifer was created to dwell eternally in the throne room of heaven, in the very presence of God (Ezekiel 28:14).

So he offers counterfeit realities to frustrate God's plan for your life. In fact his pride is what caused him to be the first counterfeit which return, reduced him to satan also known as the devil. He wanted to usurp who he was created to worship, and that is God. Being full of himself he tried to exalt his throne above God. Instead, he was slammed out of heaven as fast as lightning to the earth. He once excelled in beauty, now; he is the lowest among creation and never able to worship God again. So, he offers you imitations to keep you from worshiping the real deal, Jesus Christ.

Some counterfeits look authentic. You cannot tell it is a fake by looking at it with the natural eye. When you walk into the store and hand the cashier a $100 bill, they use wisdom to distinguish fake from real. They hold it up to the light because the light will expose the counterfeit. Psalms 119:105 says your word is a lamp for my feet, a light on my path. Had it not been for the word of God, I never would have known I was worshiping a counterfeit. The light exposes the lie and expels darkness. The use of wisdom and understanding will reveal countless counterfeits such as: money, religion, jobs, material stuff, relationships, reputations, and if your heart is lifted up with pride like satan YOU could be the counterfeit that keeps you from heaven;

never being able to worship God. My counterfeit was gang affiliation. A need for love, acceptance, and purpose have thousands of young people killing and dying prematurely because they are worshiping a counterfeit that cannot deliver.

People from all walks of life; young and old alike are worshiping counterfeits. Some of them will never pick up a bible. We may be the only light they see; which will expose their counterfeits. We, the true worshipers who worship God in spirit and truth; we who are the children of promise (Israel) through faith in Jesus Christ, are to declare His name throughout all the earth. We must declare that there is no gang, no hood, no city, no god like Jehovah. All the glory and honor belongs to Him. He alone is to be worshiped; nothing else; no one else.

The next day I went to the yard and denounced blood. I told the brothers," I cannot be a part of this no more. I cannot have nothing before God, I'm going all the way with Jesus." I didn't know what the outcome was going to be. I just knew I wasn't going to let nothing keep me from doing what God put in my heart. I felt alone like I was saying goodbye to a loved one forever. They were a part of me

I wished they would just come with me; but, no, I had to do this one on my own. I could see, for some of them, the love of God wasn't in their hearts and he wasn't on their agenda. Some people don't believe in Jesus, but that's on them they got their free will and I got mine.

I chose Jesus and I wasn't going back on it. If it has to be Blood in; Blood out; then so be it. They could've roughed me up but God was with me. My departure was one of grace. The only blood that had to be shed was the blood of Christ shed on Calvary over 2000 years ago.

The Visitation

Even though I left what was a part of me I felt more fulfilled. That alone feeling came and went like a shadow passing a wall. That's all it was, just a feeling. The truth is Christ will never leave me nor forsake me; now I felt closer to Christ than ever before.

Being a Christian is nothing like I thought it would be in my youth. I thought it was just a set of rules to restrict you from doing what you wanted to do. That's the devil's translation. That's probably what he got you thinking, but it's much more than that. Just to scratch the surface, it is God sending His Word to pull you from the pit of destruction.

Job 33:15-18 (NASB) reads, "In a dream, a vision of the night, when sound sleep falls on men, while they slumber in their beds, 16-then he opened the ears of men, and seals their instruction, 17-that he may turn man aside from his conduct, and keep man from pride, 18-he keeps back his soul from the pit."

Sometimes you have dreams, and you know that this is just a dream, so you think nothing much of it. Then there are times you have a dream and you know that this is not an ordinary dream; this is God. This is one of those nights God made certain that I knew it was Him.

He spoke up, in the dream. His voice came right in, like a man walking through double doors and interrupted everything. His sovereignty allows Him to go anywhere and deliver a message. Even places that exist only in your mind, He can meet you there. I've shared this dream many times and it goes like this.

It was at the time of day when night starts to slowly ease in. We were in the projects having a block party. Five of us begin to walk off. I cannot describe anyone's face I just know one had two braids going to the back, and one had plats. We were walking in the middle of the street. We had a sense of pride like we owned the streets. The music could still be heard and our hearts were lifted up like we did not have to bow down to no one.

As we walked further off the music could no longer be heard, the street began to decline, and now we are walking down and an unfamiliar street. On each side of the street there was nothing but darkness. It was so dark that each side of the street was like a wall of darkness. Nothing could be seen beyond that darkness.

Each man began to drift to the side of the street they were closest to. As each man gets close to the side of the street he vanishes as if the darkness sucked him in. The sound the darkness made when it sucked them in was like a man hitting a joint. It was swift and quick. He's there and then he is no more.

Now it's just me walking in the middle of the street. As I'm walking I see this dark shape coming at me very fast about the size of a car. I could sense the hatred in this dark shape it was so intense it didn't seem possible to hate that much. I never knew hatred to this magnitude existed. It was so intimidating that I was shook. I tried to get out the way but it was every direction I moved in. Suddlenly, I'm on this bike.

Soon as the darkness about overtook me; me and the bike lifted up; and the dark shape went right under me without stopping. Now I'm just standing there holding this bike in wonderment. Then I asked myself I wonder what would have happened if this bike would not have lifted me up. That's when the voice of God came right in this dream and said, "I will show you what would've happened, if I would not have lifted you up." I go back in time, and now I'm standing here in my recent past watching myself come down the street. Like one of my favorite old movies back to the future. Next here comes the dark shape coming at me with great speed just like before. I stand there and watch the dark shape overtake me and the bike. I saw myself die.

Never in my wildest dreams did I think I would ever be standing over myself; watching my body lay lifeless, but there I was; eyes open with no life in them. Immediately I woke up. (Mentally I never went back to sleep).

I sat straight up on my bunk, and began to think about what incident the Lord could be talking about. One incident stood out the most. That night a close homie was murdered and I got locked up. A week later I made bond.

I stayed out long enough to hear Keysha Key say, "Beno, you were supposed to be dead that night, they were trying to get you, John Doe said he was aimed right at you and don't know how he missed." Then I got locked right back up the next day. How she found out is not important, but the way she said it. Her eyes were wide and focused in on me. She had an expression like she just knew it was a miracle and she said it with such conviction; like it was important for me to know that.

Some people may think foolishly like I once did. Your response may be, no big deal, we all got to die one day. The problem with that is back then I wasn't fit to die. If I go now, it's all good, I'll be carried by the angels into a blessed place, but back then I would have been dragged by demons into a cursed place. Nothing I lived for had any redeeming value.

If that would have been me that night, then I would have went to hell and none of my homeboys had any authority to come down there and get me out. Today, I would still be in never ending torment. R.I.P Beno would do nothing to ease that. Condolences do not help; nothing but the blood of Jesus. So, I understand that, but what I didn't understand about the dream is the bike. Why was it in the dream?

If it was with me when I went up, and it was with me when I went down what purpose did it serve? That's when God made it clear. In your heart you thought you were still alive because of your guns and your homeboys but look how many gang members are dead now. Cursed is the one who trust in man, who draws strength from mere flesh and whose heart turns away from the Lord. (Jeremiah 17:5) That bike is like people lives. I did not use that bike to lift you up I lifted you up to pull the bike up. Today you're only living to save life or you yourself would be dead.

I want to make sure it's understood that this truth encounter did not come in an audible voice. I clarify the times I hear from God in an audible voice because it is very seldom. Most of the times I hear from God it is not in an audible voice. It's simply an understanding He puts in my heart from knowing His word. I know it's Him because I know His word.

This time I heard God with my heart. I know in my heart He's not telling me walking with Him means run off and leave my brothers, sisters and their children in the condition they're in. What kind of man gets pulled from the pit of destruction, only to walk off leaving others in there? I cannot do it or I will die. Purpose is what saved me and purpose is what's keeping me alive. Now, if I extend my hand, but you choose to stay in there, then I've done my part. Your blood is on your hands, not on mine.

So, making a change does not mean you have deserted your brothers instead you have become a lifesaver. It does not mean you do not love them anymore it means you love them according to knowledge. I know too much now to laugh and joke about the things we did yesterday. I would never celebrate our death or encourage your destruction.

Now that's love. It does not hurt them for you to think with sound judgment.

Understand love for someone should not cause you to hate a multitude of people that look just like us. Tell me my brother how can I say I love you if I teach you hate. If you asked me for a fish what kind of man would I be if I handed you a snake. The snake represents the devil and destruction, the author of confusion.

Confusion means lack of understanding or uncertainty, which is derived from walking in darkness; darkness meaning ignorance. If I ask you for some bread and you turn around and give me a stone. That might not necessarily mean you don't love me could just mean you are ignorant. Either or whatever this relationship is derived from it is killing us both.

Somebody has to wise up now because death and destruction is never satisfied it will take you, your loved ones and everybody else. Learn to test words like you taste food. There is a way that seems right to a man, but its end is destruction. Know the value of life before it is gone.

Understand, it is incomparable to anything on earth. There is nothing weak about asking your brother to put the gun down and let's pray about it. If I can't help you to be the best man you can be, if you can't help me to be the best man I can be, then what's the nature of this relationship? Who sent you?

As iron sharpens iron man sharpens man you need a brother that is going to hold you accountable, not a yes boy. I love change I know it was necessary for me to live. I'm blessed to have made a change but I know every man needs it. No one is above change but God.

Although change is good for you; what makes it great is when you are able to impact others to change for the better. The only competition we should have is in who can love the hardest. No matter where a person is from, what affiliation they claim, what race they are, if your life results in saving a life you have reached the essence of life.

Power to be the Change

Acts 1:8

But you will receive power when the Holy Spirit has come upon you;
and you shall be my witnesses in Jerusalem and in all Judea and
Samaria and even the remotest part of the earth.

These events all happened in chronological order. I did my time at a FCI in Manchester Kentucky. This place was a spiritual powerhouse. There were brothers there on fire for the Lord. These brothers inspired me. They knew the word and we built each other up daily with it.

We won souls and discipled them in the ways of Christ; because we were together every day. There were two well-known Christian men, brother Allen and brother Henning, who were leaders among the brethren. Brother Allen had the fruit of the Spirit. The way he interacted with people and treated them was inspiring. Brother Henning had the knowledge and could deliver it powerfully.

One day we had a meeting in the chapel. The teaching was on the baptism of the Holy Spirit. After the lesson, several of us stood up to receive the baptism. I lifted my hands with desire and asked the Lord to fill me. I told God I wanted more.

When I noticed I was praying in tongues I started jumping up and down with excitement. That was the best day of my life ever. No other day will match that. Right there, in the penitentiary. Nothing will ever compare with the day I was filled with the Holy Ghost. That's the day I got a praise that shakes hell.

Later that evening as I was walking back to the pod, I looked up to the sky smiling at God. The night was aflame with stars. From the top of my lungs, I shouted out hallelujah! That praise was full of Thanksgiving. I started thinking to myself, how did I get like this? How did I get here? Then I said to the Lord, "thank you for allowing me to get locked up. There is no way I would be where I am at now, if this would not have happened; if God did not allow me to be locked up. Thank you Lord, for the policemen who caught me!

To the policemen who caught me; bless them and their family. Had they not caught me, Lord where would I be?"

Now I can see the results of my prayers for change. It's not just in my heart. I could actually see the manifestation of my faith in my everyday life. Spiritually, mentally, and physically; I'm a better man for it.

A year later I was tested; I didn't see it coming. A man from up North made a slick comment. I never even had a conversation with this man before. I didn't know the man and he didn't know me. This man did not know how I used to get down. Evidently, I had been in some conversation of his that caused him speculation about me.

One day I was walking by and he looked at me with disgust and said, "sometimes you got to fake it to you make it don't you." Then he started laughing and being silly. I stopped, and for a second his head started looking real good. You know that feeling you get right before you are about to swing at what's in focus. No sooner than that feeling came it was replaced.

66

After taking a good look at him I immediately knew what it was. I noticed something about him that made me feel compassion for him. He really didn't know. How can he understand my zeal, and my commitment? In a place like this if he had never experienced what I experienced, he can't see what I see so it doesn't look real to him.

It seemed to him, like I was doing too much, because he had not tasted the goodness of God. Truth is he just needed to see Jesus. He needed exactly what I needed; that which had won me over. He needed mercy, not a beat down.

I loosened up, then I told him, "I'll be praying for you man" and walked off. When I walked away, the power of change felt so much better, than anything I'd felt throughout the times, when I would respond to disrespect with insults and violence. This freedom changed the way I viewed offenses from then on. Walking away may seem weak to some men, but even the weakness of God is far greater than the power of man.

Offenses are going to come regardless; no matter what you do. Ask God ahead of time for understanding.

Do not respond to every insult with another insult. It is to a man's glory to overlook an offense, but if the wise man argues with the fool then no one will know which one is the fool. Besides, he was not the only one who felt that way.

I knew something was in the air, but I was not going to let it stop me. People I didn't even know in the penitentiary were saying that when I get out I was going to start back banging. When I got out, people I knew said I would be locked right back up in a few months.

Outside of the men of faith, the only men that believed it was real to the point that they showed love and encouragement were PI Thomas and Pinecone. I appreciate them and I'm there for them when they need me. Love always homies, both of you are in my prayer book. I am determined to see you in heaven.

A Job and a Church

My time of departure had come. The penitentiary had served its purpose and I served my time well. Now it is time to see if it's real. Indeed, the truth is about to come out because the true test is beyond the fence. (Shout out to David may God bless the work of your hands it's all for His glory) Decisions you make any time in life count, but the ones you make out here affect you the most. These decisions are the big dictators of your life. These decisions determine if you will live or die; be victorious or defeated. You can mean well, and you can try, but good intentions don't hold up under pressure.

Just being real alone doesn't get it, you can be real and ignorant at the same time. God said (Hosea 4:6) my people are destroyed for lack of knowledge. Not a lack of income, lack of opportunities or lack of realness but a lack of knowledge.

I often hear people say," just because I do not go to church does not mean I am not a real Christian. Indeed, it does not; but it could mean you are an ignorant Christian.

The wise understand that there are some people you really do need to stay away from; but we all need somebody. Forsake not the assembling of ourselves. (Hebrews 10:25)

The first two things I looked for when I came home were a job and a church home. Those two were top priorities. I didn't give myself any other option but to work. I live by the rules; if a man don't work, he doesn't eat. On day one when man took his first breath, the first thing God said to him is, "be fruitful." That means produce. That ought to resonate in your brain if you don't work you might as well stamp an 'out of order' sign on your forehead and let it be known you can't produce. I was determined to get a job. I knew someone was going to hire me. My backup plan had backup plans; plan ABCDE until I get a job.

In two weeks I had a job and I was in church. The feeling of being in church was beautiful. I waited years for this. The Church was more than what I thought it would be. I saw people that were on dope, set free and their life restored. I saw former dope boys and hustlers living for the Lord.

About a month in the halfway house I was able to get out for a day. So I went to visit my dad. We had a grown man conversation. By now he had been married for years to a beautiful lady named Gwen. My dad wasn't just going to church and playing that bass guitar; now he was walking with God.

My dad was a big man with big arms, but he was a humble man. He embraced me and said, "I'm sorry I failed you guys." I said, "You're not to blame, everyone falls at times but that doesn't make us a failure if we get back up. We both fell but thank God we didn't fall into destruction. You stepping up when you did made a big difference in my life. If you wouldn't have stepped up when you did, it could've been a different outcome than now. I owe you a thank you dad. I appreciate you now."

"Truth is you all saved my life when I took you in, I have a history too," he told me. I said I heard about it in the state penitentiary. Then I cracked a smile and said do you remember your home boys Willie Lee and Flutie? Dad, with a light chuckle said, "yep, those were the old days"

My dad was encouraged by my change, it meant a lot to him. He wanted me to meet his Pastor from Francistown, Botswana Southern Africa. He wrote a book called the 24 Doctrines of the Bible, and is the Founder of Good News Bible College.

Indeed, I was ready to meet this man that traveled all over the world doing ministry. My dad said he was a strong man of God. I thought a big dark skinned Mandingo warrior was about to walk in the room, but an old white man walked in and said, hi Kwabena. I thought to myself okay, he doesn't look like an African then responded, Hey Mr. Wooldridge.

When he shook my hand I notice even though he didn't look like a warrior he had a grip like one.

When he shook my hand he held onto it, looked me in

the eyes and said, "Where you are going to church, the only thing you are going to do is sit. God didn't call you to go to church and just sit." I said, okay, but I didn't tell him how I really felt. I knew God had more for me to do than just sit, but I was comfortable sitting. It was hard to get past God using me while dealing with social anxiety, it was like facing a giant.

A Broken Heart That Can Endure

We all have chapters in our lives, we don't care to talk about, but those are probably the episodes people can learn the most from. Pain, suffering, and disappointment, does not pass over the Christian; we have to go through it.

There is no way around it, but if you do not give up there is a better you waiting on the other side. Inwardly, we come out of storms worth more than we were worth before we went into the storm. Elohim's creation speaks volumes on this topic. Elohim is the name used for God during creation, (Genesis 1:1). In Genesis, when the world is created, I believe the core of a diamond is created to demonstrate a perfect backdrop for the purpose of trials, and tribulations; stuff that causes pressure in our life. Without untold pressure a diamond will remain nothing but a piece of coal, but when that old dusty, flaky, oily black rock, endures indefinable pressure, the value of it increases exceedingly; so much so, its name, its course, and the essence of its purpose changes.

It is now called a diamond; now, it is no longer tossed on the ground or thrown into a fireplace to be burned for fuel. It is put into a showcase for everyone to see how beautiful and valuable it is; now, it is to be desired. I've learned not to trust giving my heart to someone who have not been through a storm and stayed committed to the purpose.

Have you ever had something special in life that you wanted to share with someone that was special to you? Faith is a matter of the heart; to share my faith with a woman, is to share my heart. To have someone that loves God as much as you do or more. To have someone to pray with, study the word of God with, willing to turn their back to the world and become one flesh in the ministry. In my eyes this is how you make love.

I figured if we save the sex for marriage God would bless it forever. I call it anointed lovemaking even though it's too late for us to be virgins; we can still be the best that each other has ever had. What can the devil do with a spiritual powerhouse like this? Nothing! But get crushed. All of hell would be afraid of a relationship like this. The enemy and his cohorts would try to do anything to prevent this from happening. I gave it a try but I was too anxious.

Being around all of them hard ankles for years, I came out ready to jump into something. I held off on sex until I got married, but I rushed for the Altar. Not realizing that everyone doesn't have the same mindset for marriage. Some people look at marriage from a different perspective.

There are several facets to a marriage; to some marriage is a business. Some people may see that as the key element in a marriage. In fact, it's common; to each their own choice. Indeed, business minded collaboration is important, but it's not the heartbeat of a marriage to me. Everyone have their own expectations which, I believe should be expressed openly and frankly; all of the whys and what fore's you are looking for in a marriage.

If I would've slowed it down and been more analytical, I would have realized, even though my heart was right, I was not ready for a marriage. All I could bring to the table was a Bible and $300 on a good month. I was in school full-time and working part-time with a car payment. I was ready for some of them benefits, but I didn't know what I was getting myself into. This was my first relationship, and there had not been a prototype in our home. My mom and dad had never been together in my life-time. I didn't even know how to talk to a wife.

I figured if a man would never cheat on his woman then that was the indicator that he was ready for marriage. At first everything was looking smooth when I got married. I was in school and I was due to graduate in 18 months. The part-time job I had was heating and air repair. It was in the same field I was going to school for. I would've graduated with two years of on the job experience; which means I would have graduated as an experienced HVAC technician. That would have started me out with decent pay from the day of graduation.

I took a walk down that aisle; right after the honeymoon, I walked into a four bedroom house with a two car garage. Never, before this time, had I ever lived in something like this. Pulling up in garages and walking on hardwood floors is something I had only seen on TV from a prison cell.

I wrote my brothers in the penitentiary to give them an update. Everyone was inspired, they were so encouraged; their faith was strengthened in knowing and believing that God can make a way for them too, when they come home. It felt good strengthening my brothers, who all shared the same struggle. To be able to contribute to someone's growth that had contributed so much to mine was an honor. Until this day, I still have all the letters they wrote. Several of them sent pictures with their bibles and a tank top on, wanting me to set them up with a woman of God.

Suddenly, what seemed to be a blessing, sorrowfully, began to become regretful. I didn't have the respect as a provider there in that home; and I didn't deserve it. I walked into a kingdom that was already established before I got there; a family that was already broken with three beautiful daughters who were still healing because they missed their father. Their daddy told me to my face," from the first time I looked at you I hated you for staying in a house that I bought with my family."

I understood how he felt. I didn't buy anything in that

house, he built that kingdom. At one time he paid all the bills and for the time I was there, I could barely pay the utilities. I was living in a house and sleeping on stuff that he worked to buy. As a man, I understood that so I never got offended. I always respected that man and saluted him for being a good father. It was not long at all before I started feeling a sense of unworthiness in that place. I was never given a door key the entire time I lived there. I always came in through the garage door. Two months after I got married all of my plans started to crumble right before my eyes. I was working for A&C heating and air, owned by a good man. He was not making the profit margin he needed, to keep me on board, so he had no choice but to let me go.

I was in school for eight hours a day but, most of what I learned came from working at A&C heating and air. I could not find a part-time job to correspond with my school schedule. Now school was coming to an end. That's when the bottom fell out of my marriage and It wasn't looking good for me career wise either. Being a two-time felon, it just didn't seem like I had many options to find work that could provide a good life.

My wife's girlfriend asked her, " What were you thinking about when you married that? The only thing he ever had on his own was a jail cell." But, of course, she was having problems in her marriage too. I started working two jobs. One of them was at the Rush as a personal trainer; nice, profession, but it wasn't paying much. The problem with this job is that you do not get paid unless you are training. It could take a while to build up enough clientele to reach full time.

I was written up twice; Once for talking to a client about Jesus; the second write up was for asking my client if she wanted prayer, both of them sold me old, and dropped the dime on me, so they would not give me any clients because Jesus is not part of a professional environment.

I was hired on another job at Propak logistics, a warehouse job, where they rebuild pallets and distribute them out around the nation. It was a dusty and sweaty job. I came home dirty every day. It didn't pay much, but it was 40 hours most weeks, although sometimes they sent us home early. With another job I was able to earn more, but this didn't help my marriage. Lord knows, I tried, but to no avail.

One day I came home from work and the garage door was locked. I went to the front door and it was locked as well. I knocked on the door, that's when my wife opened up the window and said, "Go away Kwabena, nobody wants you here."

I had dreams of being a great husband. When I was in the penitentiary I told God," when you give me my queen I will be the best servant king in this world to her, second only to you Lord." I was zealous; I studied to know my duties as a husband to be a prophet, priest and king. How is it I'm standing here on this porch and I'm told I'm not even wanted by anyone in this house? The people I love the most are in there. Undeniably, I was heartbroken.

I didn't want to believe it but I knew it was coming to an end, just not like this. It is cold out here. At least care enough to give me time to get situated. This made it hurt all the more, but I see this is how it really is; I cannot force anyone here to care. I left thinking someone would let me in somewhere but no one did. Some family members didn't even believe my change was real. They figured now that my marriage failed I'm going to go back to the penitentiary; it's just a matter of time. It was expected of me to fail; no one had ever seen anything else.

I never had my own place. I was only out of the halfway house for two months before I got married. I had no track record of making it on my own. I called my dad he wanted to help, but could not let me in. I felt like I didn't have anybody in this world. I drove out to the country and parked at an old abandoned church my granddad preached at before I was born.

Right there, I camped in my car. I didn't feel comfortable sleeping in the open. I feared someone might try to take my life as a trophy, simply because of my past. I just sat there in my car, it was pitch-black. I was hurt, alone, and confused. Last year I had a lot of brothers encouraged by my life; somewhat of an inspiration to them and now this. It felt like God was playing games with me. I said, "God I did it your way. I didn't even have sex with her until we got married, but

I'm the one that ends up getting crushed."

Although I am a changed man; decisions I made in the past are still making it really hard for me today. I thank God for change, but the process is really making me think about going back right about now. My thoughts were contradicting my heart. I felt a certain way one minute, then another way the next, as if I was bipolar.

The next morning I drove to work I went straight to the restroom, fixed myself up, and started working. After work I went to The Rush, (the gym) I worked out, took a shower, got something to eat, then I went and parked in that old abandoned church my granddad once preached at; reading my favorite Greek and Hebrew keynote study Bible, until I went to sleep.

This was my routine for a little over two weeks, until I was able to save up a couple of checks to rent an apartment. By now, I had been out of church for three weeks.

As much as I loved the church I was going to. I thought it was more important for my wife to be going there than me.

She was not in church when I met her. I led her to the Lord and I wanted her to keep that. I thought to myself something good has to come out of this. Her eternal security would be worth everything we went through, we can't lose that. I was in on that so I felt protective. It was a blessing to be a part of that.

I truly believe I was supposed to be her big brother spiritually, and a personal trainer maybe, but not a husband. I was not going to let her leave on my account, and I was not about to stay there and risk seeing her move on. I left that church feeling a little discouraged; thinking I would not find a church as good as the one I was attending.

A brother who went to the same church I was attending and he lived in the same apartment building I just moved into. He welcomed me to the neighborhood. He noticed I'd been out of church for a while so he asked me, "Is everything alright." I know he had good intent, so I told him my situation. He said he had been to Overcomer Believers Church and it's a good church. It is like the one we go to. At first I thought, how does he know for sure? Is he just being optimistic and making good conversation. I didn't know anyone who goes to that church to confirm what he was saying. Two months went by and I was still not connected. I was in church limbo. I didn't know where to go. I visited a couple of churches, but I felt like I could teach those Pastors.

One Friday I came home from work and everything just hit me. I started feeling lonely. I thought to myself I got to get out of this place I can't sit in here stressing. Figured I'd get out and help my mind switch topics. I drove through to see what the brothers were doing from the neighborhood. I came across a homeboy named J-Stroll. I told him my situation he said, " Shake it off homie you been doing good out here bruh and you will keep winning.

I know you are changed man blood; I know what you come from; God got you."

I already knew what he was saying was true and it felt good being around love. That alone was encouraging, but to hear J-Stroll talk about God and change like that, was an even bigger blessing. So, I replied with, "brother it is a blessing to hear you talk like that, it sounds to me like you have faith too."

He said, "I'm not a fool. I always believed in God. I know He been watching over for me too." After a five seconds pause he say, we about to go to a new place that just opened up off Chapman Highway, do you want to ride? I told him I would follow them down there.

When we got down there I see it had a nice crowd. While we were still in line some words got exchanged with some brothers I heard were from Miami. Then a scuffle broke out right there in line. I call myself going to break it up and one of those dudes just took off on me and hit me in the jaw. I grabbed the dude by his collar snatched him to me, picked him up and threw him through the glass wall. Then I heard a voice say, "You're back."

I froze for a second, then I looked around me as if I was just now aware of what is really going on, I said, "no." Without saying another word to anyone I left. I got in my car and drove home. I opened up the door. As soon as I walked in, I fell on my knees and asked for forgiveness. I remember finishing my prayer with this, "Father keep me and don't let me go, don't let me slip back. You said in your word the good work You started in me You will complete it 'til the end, and I will be ready for the coming of Jesus Christ in Jesus name Amen."

I didn't know whose voice that was back there that said 'you're back'. Was that God or was it the enemy's voice? I said it can't be God's voice because that's a lie and devil you are the liar. I am nothing like what I used to be, and I don't even miss being that. Yes I'm feeling alone right about now. I miss the love, the unity, and the acceptance, but I'm far from being a gangster.

Yes, I love these brothers and I always will, love is not going anywhere, but I love Jesus Christ way much more; period, point blank; there is no competition there. I wish I could win them all over to Christ that's the realest thing a man can do for his homies. However, It simply does not get as real as Jesus; nobody will do for you what He has done. They can't even qualify. If I have to walk alone then so be it. This can't last forever anyway.

Back in Church

The next day I came across Kevin again at Walmart. The first words that came out of his mouth was did you go visit Overcoming Believers Church yet. I said, I haven't yet blessed man, but I do need to get connected somewhere ASAP. He said, you should go check it out man. I'm telling you Beno you will be blessed. I told myself okay I'm going, but I'm not going to pay my tithes until I get out the hole.

I got up the next day threw on some jeans, tennis shoes, a button up shirt and went out the door. When I got to the building I had to drive around for a while to find a parking space. It took me longer to find a parking space than it did for me to get there. When I walked in the building just about the whole church were on their feet praising and worshiping the Lord. Five minutes later a brother named Chris pulled up right beside me.

I had just met this brother downtown two weeks ago. We clicked as soon as we met. Both of us shared our testimony with one another. Talking about how King Jesus saved us and what He delivered us from. We both had similar backgrounds and we knew God was calling us to step up. We talked for an hour about God and change in the middle of the city directly across the street from the movie theater near downtown market Square.

I was glad to see him going to this church. I asked him how long have you been going here. He said this was his first time visiting. We both watched as the Pastor came out. An ole skinny guy, he looked kind of young for a Pastor but when he preached he got in my business.

I said I was not going to pay my tithes until I get out the whole. My first day here Pastor said, "faith doesn't do right only when it's convenient. Robbing God is not going to get you back on your feet."

I didn't come to hear that today, but I knew he was right, I was convicted. I started checking myself, thinking, "I cannot rob my source what am I thinking. Do I really believe the word of God works? I can't hold back on God when it gets tough. Are we friends or what?

Even when I was in the streets I never robbed anybody I was cool with and now that I have a friend that sticks closer to me than a brother I'm about to rob Him. No not today, not after hearing this Pastor." Man I wanted to go up there and hug little dude after that word, but I didn't want to draw any attention to myself. I tried to avoid too much interaction.

I really didn't want to be known. My confidence was shot and I didn't want to be exposed with these social anxieties I been dealing with; not In front of all of these new people. I just wanted to come to church to sit, listen, and heal. Evidently, God had other plans. I didn't have time to get comfortable. The Word would not let me.

My fourth Sunday there Pastor got in my business again, preaching Kingdom business. He said it's more to walking with God than just coming to a church building on Sundays. You know God called you to do more than just sit in the sweet seat. I was convicted. It was as if he was up in my face talking to me.

I knew I would be in rebellion if I did not do something

and rebellion can get ugly. It is a dangerous state to be in. Rebellion is as the sin of witchcraft according to scripture. Check this verse out, 1 Samuel 15:23 reads "for rebellion is as the sin of witchcraft and stubbornness is as iniquity and idolatry. Because you have rejected the word of the Lord He has also rejected you from being king." So after service I went to the front and introduce myself to Minister Shawn Watkins. I told her I was ready to help out then I asked her do you have any bathrooms that need to be cleaned? She just smiled and said, "come with me." I followed her and she introduced me to Pastor Daryl Arnold.

From that day forward I was connected. I had accountability and phenomenal leadership. He embraced me and became a father to me in the faith. The following Sunday I sat in the front and started learning how to serve as an Armor Bearer.

I had to face this fear and insecurity that comes from having a social anxiety; a strategic attack from the enemy against my mind. I continue to overcome this by learning to serve. I say overcome and not overcame because it is a continued victory. As long as I keep a servant's heart I have victory in this area.

A mind that is self-consumed is self-destructive. Being too self-conscious can create anxiety. I did not know this at first. I learned this over time. There were times I tried to get out of serving because of my insecurities but serving was the very thing God was using to heal and deliver me.

Now I understand breakthroughs don't always come from an altar call. I believe most likely they will come from our obedience. A Servant's heart is priceless. Serving is **one of the best decisions I ever made in my life, but having the privilege to serve a king** and a general in the faith such as my Pastor Daryl Arnold is the highest honor God has giving me on this earth.

Not long after being connected to the body of Christ, God Almighty, who is all-knowing, started speaking to another member on my behalf. One Sunday a prophetess name Karren told me she heard from God and I need to listen. She said, "Your wife is closer to you than you think but she is not ready, God is still doing a work in her. Your ex-wife is going to try diligently to come back to you. You can take her back if you want to and you will miss what God really has for you." Then she just walked off without saying another word. I thought to myself I know Carren mean well but she got to be mistaken on this one. The way my ex-wife dumped me there is no way that woman sees anything in me I am nothing to her.

Then six months later it happened just as she said it would. Of course I was tempted to go back that was the only woman I've ever been in love with, but that prophetic word kept me from going in that direction.

Being connected to the body of Christ will keep us from making life altering decisions that could hinder our destiny or set us back. Not that she is a bad person but I am to marry for purpose and love. I knew right then, if the first part the prophetess said was true then, the second part is as well, so while God is getting my wife ready for me.

I committed to getting things ready for her including myself. Now after the honeymoon all we have to do is walk into our kingdom and can't anybody ever take anything from us, because we own it.

Three weeks after I met Pastor we started walking through the projects with two of the other Armor Bearers or better yet disciples Chris and Eric we were witnessing and loving on the people in the neighborhood. I observed his people skills. People he just met, he was talking to them and connecting with them like he knew them for years.

Indeed there was work to be done. The following year, it seemed more children died in Knoxville than any year before. We could not help but notice because we were burying almost all of them. They were coming to us funeral after funeral; child after child I had to stand there and watch those children lay in them caskets. One of them was our very own Eli.

Eli took a liking to me because I was someone he could relate to. His roots are from Ohio where his father and mother were Crips. His mother was delivered and gave her life to Christ. So naturally he had a taste for gang life but he also had vision. Sometimes his mind would war between the two.

He had a plan to get a scholarship in sports to go to college, but he also wanted to be a part of something right now. Every weekend my house was his house. After I made sure he was taking care of business like he was supposed to, then we would kick it and have some fun. I would show him how to work out, and I would show him how to box.

He used to love that stuff, he was a natural athlete. One Sunday in church Chris looked over his shoulder at the altar and he noticed that the Holy Spirit was moving on Eli. So we walked over there and started ministering to him. Right then he was born again and filled with the Holy Spirit.

Exactly two weeks later from that day on a Sunday night, we were in my living room fellowshipping on Linden Avenue. I said Eli let's walk outside for a minute the sky was lit up with stars. I said Eli look up, you see those stars how they sit there perfectly and never move out of place. There is not a Crip or Blood in this world that can do that but our God. God upholds all things by the power of His word.

If we are going to be like anybody we are going to be like Him. We are just like Him; value life, no matter whose it is. We value life. He said Beno when I get out of high school I want to study law enforcement. I want to be a detective. I said don't you let anybody tell you there's anything wrong with that. We need some good people in those positions with a heart to protect us; someone who values life. I had no idea that this would be our last conversation my last time seeing him.

Tuesday night I got a call in the middle of the night. As soon as I heard that phone ring I felt something wasn't right. It was Chris he told me to get to the hospital Eli has been shot. I got there as fast as I could but he was gone home before I could get there.

Eli never owned a gun, never shot a man, and never joined a gang. He was walking home from school after football practice. Some of his schoolmates that were gang affiliated, called him over to talk with them. They first won his trust, and then they walked him through an alley and shot him in the back. The bullet hit him in the heart.

This death wasn't just close to home but it was in my home. I was bereaved and mad at the same time. I didn't understand his untimely death. Eli was supposed to be one of our champions. He was going to break the mode. In spite of all the troubles and temptations that surround the youth with gangs, drugs and violence he was going to show them how not to give in. He had courage to stand out.

Instead he was killed by another child looking for acceptance and found it in the arms of a counterfeit (the devil) that can't even stand his very existence; because he was created in the image of God to be like God and worship the most high God. So the child took on the image of a counterfeit that hates him and Eli (the devil).

Now Eli's death is like a trophy to him and his life has no more value than an oily rag laying in the street all because of a color. Kids killing kids (KKK) over a color is the same ideology as the Ku Klux Klan. Today I can see how that is as stupid as the hell it came from, but at one time I could not see because that spirit had me bound too. These spirits are clever and good at what they do.

They have an army that moves In Sync. They have been around for a long time and they know how to stay off your radar. You cannot identify the problem without the word of God. No man or child has a chance with them alone; but greater is He that is in me than he that is in the world. I know the power of God can set any man free because I know what He did in me and He is no respecter of persons. What He did in me He can do in any man.

So I'll fight back with my testimony, the blood of the Lamb and the word of God. I'm not letting this ride. This problem is widespread, it's been in my face and now it just walked up in my home. I had to do something, ready or not it is war. In my time of bereavement God gave me a word concerning Eli; Psalms 63:3 "Because your loving kindness is better than life, my lips will praise You." (NASB)

Talking about an in-season word; now, that was encouraging. What I got from that is, although they took his life they could not take his testimony. In spite of everything going on around him, at age seventeen, he chose Jesus Christ when it was not popular to do so; when it was not considered cool; he still chose the Son of God.

The fog could not stop him from seeing the light. Now Eli dwells in the house of the Lord forever, in a place prepared for him by the Lord. Nothing in this life can top that. My dad in the faith, Pastor Daryl Arnold preached his home going service. On that day 200 young people received Jesus Christ as Lord and savior. Every Austin East high school football player there was born again. That day we kicked a hole in the devil's head.

Ready or Not it's War

After Eli's Home-going service we brought the war to the devil's front porch. I started mentoring brothers in and out of Knoxville; as many as God would put in my pathway. Young brothers who were serious about change, I would go to their OG on their behalf. I would share with them the plans this young brother envisioned, to make a life for him and perhaps a family one day.

I would respectfully ask if he could take this man off roll call. I would vouch for him; he would not be in the streets playing games, but at work or school taking care of business, so he could one day provide an honest living for himself and his family. One of the young brother's with such a vision married in early 2017 to a young lady that use to gang bang herself.

For young women, it could be much more challenging when I speak with their OG's, because of the deep feelings involved. The OG could be possessive, like the girl is property that belonged to him. As long as I knew she was serious, I would stand by her and let him know that this is my sister and she is not by herself. One such young lady, was an active member at Overcoming Believers Church, had later graduated from Job Corps, so she could have great potential to successfully make an honest living.

My dad in the faith, Pastor Daryl Arnold, introduced me to Mayor Madeline Rogero. Personally, this lady is a blessing to me. I respect her as a human being and I'm thankful for her leadership in Knoxville, Tennessee. She serves this city without partiality and without prejudice.

She is a pillar of support for building the Change Center in Knoxville, Tennessee.

The Change Center is a safe haven for inner-city youth to study, work, have fun, and be mentored by God fearing leaders. Some people grumbled about the mayor spending hundreds of thousands of dollars on a center that is not going to fix all the problems.

Realistically, the change center is not a panacea, but it is a great stride toward improvement. If it saves only one child, it would mean the world to the parent whose child was saved as a result of the existence of the Change Center.

In 2013 Mayor Rogero united with mayors all across the nation, in the 'Cities United', and began the Save Our Sons initiative. This initiative is a city wide effort to eliminate violent deaths among boys and young men of color, as well as increasing opportunities for their success.

At a Knoxville City Convention, Mayor Rogero allowed me the privilege and opportunity to be a keynote speaker. After speaking I met Police Chief, David B. Rausch, a man I believe God placed in that position. I believe men like him will aid in healing the broken relationships between inner city communities and the police departments that are assigned to protect and serve those communities.

He was extremely encouraging after hearing my testimony. He said, he prayed that what happened for me would happen for more people in our city. In church we have the same mission, but what he does for the police department is his job; that is where the line is drawn. My work is different, I try to reach a man before somebody else judges him. I do this through leading by example. I respect the law and I love living right; not because I am worried about going to jail, but because God has written his laws upon my heart.

I assure you of this, because of the Spirit of God who is within me. I am just as ethical as the man who never made the mistakes that I have made. Never looking at any man as being better than me, neither, I as being better than any man, but accepting myself as a flawed human being made righteous through Jesus Christ. I am not a spokesman for politicians either. However, I do not take lightly the opportunities given me to meet people from various walks of life. I count it a blessing. It has helped mature me and expanded my vision.

Heal The Land

In these end times you never know what you'll see when you turn the news on. I'd say just about every city have local stories on the news that make you stop everything you are doing and just watch. The more you see, the more you know that things are about to get real ugly.

That is exactly how I felt the morning I seen this story on the news. It started off with someone's mother getting shot in her own house. She didn't know anything about gangs. She didn't run the streets; too busy working full-time to make a living. She makes it back home after a long day's work; ready to relax, but end up getting shot in her own house.

Minutes later an innocent teenager was killed protecting young ladies from gunfire, using his body as a human shield. The young man was a star football player for Fulton high school. He never joined a gang, he never had a gun. He was part of a program that helps save lives and promotes education. Minutes later another young man was killed. He was the son of the mother that was shot in her own home; all this happened within the same night.

Only God knows the pain these mothers felt that night. I can't even imagine or understand how they felt. I just know I would much rather be a man that helps heal the hurting, rather than be a boy that causes someone that pain.

I called Pastor up and said something has to be done right away or it is going to be another gang war that could take Knoxville back to the 90s. I told him I've been gone so long I don't even know these youngsters I'm seeing on the news it's a whole new generation out there now. I can talk to them but I can't tell them to put the guns down.

I know some OG's that know these youngsters maybe they can get them to put the guns down. We got the power but the streets got more influence over these young people than the church. It's time for the churches to meet up with the streets. He asked me if I could get them together and set up a meeting with him. I said consider it done, I went from hood to hood talking with men, who I knew were standup brothers, that have been around the block. They may not know God but they can help stop the violence; and we can teach them about God along the way. I know they're older and wiser now and they love their people enough to want better for their neighborhoods.

The next day Bloods, Crips, Gangsta Disciples, and Vice Lords were sitting up in the same room with Pastor discussing how we can fix this problem before it's too late. One of the first men who spoke was PI Thomas. He said, "Our land needs healing." We all agreed so we called the movement 'Heal the Land'.

The first plan to get the city together, we had to get in these youngsters' ears quickly. In less than 24 hours we had an emergency meeting for the city in the church building. We have a big sanctuary so Pastor opened it up to the whole city. Brothers from every side of town opened up their hearts on stage in front of the city, declaring that they were taking a stand for peace.

Some brothers humbled themselves; confessed their actions were wrong and encouraged the youngsters to do better. One brave man in a wheelchair embraced the man that put him in that wheelchair and told him I forgive you. I saw strength and virtues in brothers I never discerned in them, until that night. The joy of working with brothers and seeing men come together for good was rewarding. This was a step towards victory, but still a long ways to go.

A week goes by; tension is still high in the city, but I wasn't intimidated because men don't scare me and death doesn't discourage me. I was living on the edge when I was foolish, how much more am I willing to die like a man when it's for an honorable cause. My biggest concern was something happening to the people around me that could set them back.

I knew God was using 'Heal the Land' to heal the people that were in the movement, as much as, He was using the movement to heal the land. We walked through the projects. We started witnessing and praying for whomever would let us pray for them. Next week we followed up with another meeting. Chuck mentioned a sister he knew named, Indian McDonald, a lady that has a heart for God and her community. He said she's been holding meetings every week for a while about the same problems we're trying to fix. He recommended we link up with them.

We met up with them and could tell these sisters meant business. Indian McDonald was an expert in administrations and putting youth summits together. This expanded the vision and created more avenues to reach the youth. Pastor Daryl Arnold, already having great leadership skills, emboldens the newly formed team with inspiration.

Everyone wanted him to lead. We had more confidence with his presence, but he deferred this task to us. He said he would support us, but this is our mission. I understood him. He wanted us to have our confidence in God and learn to esteem one another more important than ourselves.

The promise that God gives us to heal the land is in 2 Chronicles 7:14; starts off saying if my people who are called by my name will humble themselves. That word if, means there is a stipulation, first you got to learn humility and respect for one another before God does anything. That's the reason we have all these problems in the land now; there is no humility and respect for one another. Now if we are going to break the mold, then the people God use definitely have to embrace this. Leaders lead by example. Be the change you want to see.

Next God mentions pray. Since we pray to God and not man our confidence is in God and not Pastors. It's only right for us to love and honor them, but understand, they get tired, they get frustrated, they hurt, and need healing too; after all they are mere men too. My Pastor often says, he is the man of God, not the God of man. There are obstacles we all have to face, problems we all encounter. We need more than good intentions to have victory, we need to walk in the power we have in Christ through prayer.

Next seek my face. People of God, He is calling out to you. He's saying put your eyes on me and see that I am to be desired. I come with healing, I am healing, reach out and touch My cloak and I will dry this issue of blood up in your land.

Next, turn from their wicked ways. God is saying the reason you need healing today is because of what you've been holding on to. Let it go. It's been making you sick for too long, but it's not too late. Turn to me and I will fix everything you messed up. I will bless you to be a blessing.

To sum it all up what God is saying is if we heal the hearts; we heal the land. Every problem we see in this land started in someone's heart first. The solution to every problem starts in someone's heart. You could be the problem or the solution we all have a choice. One or the other; is in you.

Pastor scheduled a dinner meeting with our new family so everybody could start bonding and loving on one another. We had a war ahead of us and we had to learn to be as one and move in sync. Lord knows we had a long ways to go but we had to get started because ready or not it's war.

We are the army this city needs to heal the land; Just everyday people with more heart than title. The first big movement was the grocery giveaway for the east side and the west side Lonsdale homes and Walter P Taylor homes. Absolutely everything was paid for by Overcoming Believers

Church; we had no money to do this, we just made it happen. We served each community thousands of dollars' worth of groceries.

I've experience for myself how serving can bless and mature a man. What better ways to get a break through, than to have opposing communities serve one another? Men and children from the East and the West side now providing each other what they need to live. Making the mother's in these communities smile, rather than making them cry; teaching the children that it is better to heal than to do harm. What a turn from darkness to light.

I see the joy they had in serving, because now they are experiencing the purpose that God always had for them and that is to have a servant's heart like Jesus, to Him goes the glory and the honor forever, Amen.

On Martin Luther King Day we did the traditional March through the city. We had people from different walks of life, different churches, different neighborhoods, Gangster Disciples, Vice Lords, Bloods and Crips marching together in sync with no animosity; taking a stand for love and unity.

111

Showing respect for one another building bonds that hold us together until this day.

The next week; comes the pressure, you know the stuff that makes diamonds or make you want to quit. One of our core members got the book thrown at him in court because of his past. James' sentence was enhanced by the gang law during a time when he had transformed and became a part of a movement trying to prevent gang violence. This was a discouragement to the entire inner city. So many people were pulling for him because they knew he had a renewed heart. He was not the same man he was in the 90s, but he still got railroad for it in 2016.

He was sentenced to 40 years on a drug charge. After the sentencing one young man asked me, 'Why even try to change when we still end up losing?" I told him you got more reasons to change than you do not to. He said, why? I said because God loves you. If you make a change God loves you, and if you never change God loves you. You don't change to get his love, his love makes you want to change.

If a lawyer walked in that courtroom and told James

you are free to go. I have the authority to take those handcuffs off of you and put them on me, but I will have to do your life sentence, for you to go free. As they are taking the handcuffs off of James and putting them on the lawyer. James asks the lawyer how much I owe you. The lawyer looks at James and says nothing all I want you to do is stay away from the things that got you in here; get a job, take care of your child, let her know that I love her and that I will do the same thing for her.

Now if you were James would you ask why should I change or say yes. The youngster said man I would go job hunting as soon as I left that courtroom. This lawyer I am speaking about is symbolic of a real Lord and Savior, Who went before a real Judge on our behalf.

At the closing of this book allow me to explain that His holiness is the reason Jesus Christ had to do a life sentence for our freedom. Understand that no one goes to hell because they are not good enough. No one goes to hell because God hates them. God loves everyone in hell, but his holiness will not allow anyone to be in his presence without being washed in the blood of his son Jesus Christ. God is a consuming fire. (Hebrews 12:29) You cannot enter his presence with sin. His holiness would consume you. That's why Jesus Christ had to die for us to have hope. Only his blood can take away sin according to Hebrews 10:19; therefore brothers and sisters, since we have confidence to enter the most holy Place by the blood of Jesus. Sin has to be dealt with, (judged) it cannot dwell in his presence; not in heaven or God would be an unjust God and something would happen that has never ever happened before in eternity, the holy angels would close their mouth, there would be silence, and they would cease from singing a song they had been singing since their entire existence. Revelation 4 verse eight each of the four living creatures had six wings and was covered with eyes all around, under its wings. Day and night they never stop saying, "holy, holy, holy, is the Lord God Almighty."

If God Almighty did not punish sin that would contradict what he is, and that is holy, holy, holy. In Jewish liturgy when the message is very important they put emphasis on how important it is by saying it twice Jesus himself emphasized how important a message was when he told his disciples, verily, verily I say unto you. (John 6:47, 3:3)

Now when something is mentioned three times, please take heed, stop everything you are doing and listen. Words cannot describe how important this is. Could it be that holiness is by far the most important attribute we need to know about God. The magnitude of his holiness is off the Richter scale. Sin is doomed, judgment is coming and the only way God Almighty could judge sin without destroying mankind, who is full of sin; is by putting the sins of the world on his son Jesus Christ through terrible suffering; by death on the cross. Our only escape is faith in the death, burial, and resurrection of Jesus Christ. Rejecting Jesus Christ is what sends people to hell but excepting Him as Lord and Savior is what saves us from the pit of destruction.

Conclusion

John 17:20 (NIV)

My prayer is not for them alone. I pray also for those who will believe in Me (Jesus) through their message.

As I conclude this book, I end as I began; reflecting back over my life. I realize that the end of my marriage led me back to the place which probably had the greatest impact on my salvation. It is more than ironic to me that when I was locked out of the house, tossed away like an old shoe; the place I chose to find comfort and solace was the abandoned parking lot of the old country church where my grandfather, Pastor Edward Allen Miller, used to preach.

Instinctively, I believe what I have heard people say about him; that he lived what he preached. I also believe that as he prayed for his family, even those he would never know, like me; he asked Jesus to save his family through all generations.

James 5:16 says, "Confess your faults one to another, and pray one for another, that ye may be healed. The effectual fervent prayer of a righteous man availeth much."

Like Jesus is now at the right hand of the Father interceding for the saints, I believe my grandfather made intercession for me; which is why the hand of God was over my life during my dark and foolish days. I thank him for those prayers, as I thank my biological father for interceding in our lives at a critical period of time. Had he not, God alone, knows the possibilities of me and my siblings' outcome.

My spiritual father, Pastor Daryl Arnold taught me one of the most valuable lessons I have learned in all of time. The principle of tithing, not because we have to, but because my love for Jesus and seeing His work on the cross made manifest in the lives of others, incentivizes me to want to give. I also believe being faithful in paying tithes blessed me with my own kingdom; my own place to live, the ability to supply all of my needs and some of my wants. I had the privilege of taking the man of God that sowed that very word into me on a cruise some place very far from the jail cell I cried out to God for a change in me. Understand the aspiration of a testimony, it reveals the beauty and purpose in having the power of change. What the Almighty God do for one He can do for all. Truth is He welcomes you in with alacrity. For the eyes of the Lord move to and fro throughout the earth that He may strongly support those whose heart is completely His (2 Chronicles 16:9). As loved ones prayed for me I want to pray with you. If you agree with this after you read it, read it again out loud and say amen. God Almighty holy and honored be your Name. I thank You for Jesus Christ. I believe that He died for my sins and rose up from the grave never to go back. Come into my heart and make it yours Lord. I pray that your grace abound toward everyone in my bloodline. I pray that there names be found written in the Lambs book of life. Heal the hurting and the lost in my community. Strengthen us and make us whole spiritually, mentally, and physically in Jesus name Amen.

Made in the USA
Lexington, KY
27 April 2017